A Very Blessed Easter

Activity Book

Anita Reith Stohs
Illustrated by Susan Morris

CONCORDIA PUBLISHING HOUSE • SAINT LOUIS

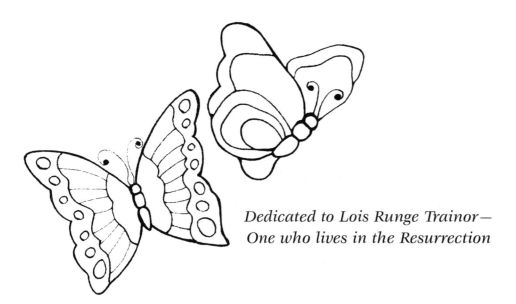

Dedicated to Lois Runge Trainor—
One who lives in the Resurrection

All Scripture quotations, unless otherwise indicated, are taken from the HOLY BIBLE, NEW INTERNATIONAL VERSION®. NIV®. Copyright © 1973, 1978, 1984 by International Bible Society. Used by permission of Zondervan Publishing House. All rights reserved.

Copyright © 1999 Concordia Publishing House
3558 S. Jefferson Avenue, St. Louis, MO 63118-3968
1-800-325-3040 • www.cph.org

Manufactured in the United States of America

8   9   10   11   12   13   14   15   17   16   15   14   13   12   11

What Is Easter?

Do you know what happened the first Easter Day? Finish this puzzle to find out why we celebrate Easter each year. Use the words in the *Word Box* to fill in the missing words from each sentence. Then find the code under each blank and write that word in the correct square of the crossword puzzle.

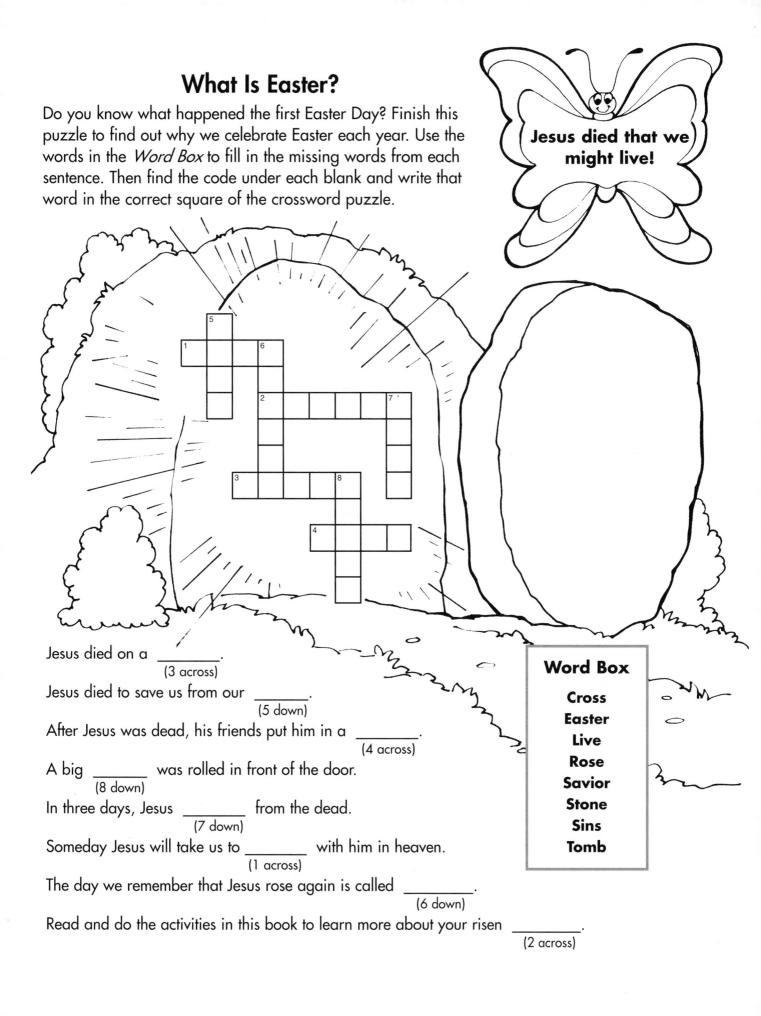

Jesus died that we might live!

Jesus died on a _____.
(3 across)

Jesus died to save us from our _____.
(5 down)

After Jesus was dead, his friends put him in a _____.
(4 across)

A big _____ was rolled in front of the door.
(8 down)

In three days, Jesus _____ from the dead.
(7 down)

Someday Jesus will take us to _____ with him in heaven.
(1 across)

The day we remember that Jesus rose again is called _____.
(6 down)

Read and do the activities in this book to learn more about your risen _____.
(2 across)

Word Box

Cross
Easter
Live
Rose
Savior
Stone
Sins
Tomb

We will live with Jesus forever.

What Easter Means

Can you find the cross in the picture puzzle below? Use your finger to trace around it. The cross reminds us that Jesus died for our sins. Now trace the circle. It has no end, and it goes around forever. The circle reminds us that the love of Jesus has no end. Because He died for our sins, we will live with Him in heaven forever.

Color the picture using bright Easter colors. Think about the beautiful colors in a stained glass window as you decorate the picture.

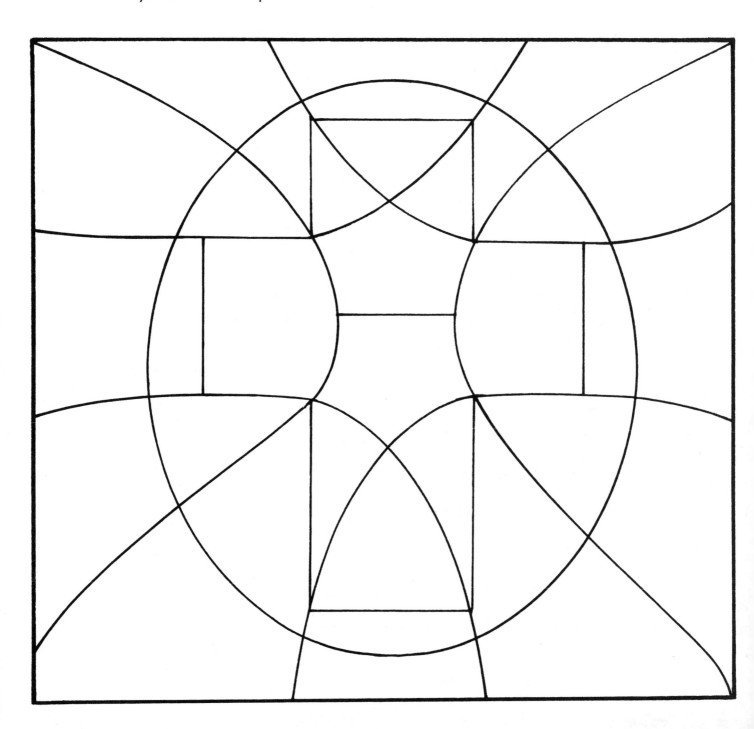

An Easter Butterfly

When we see caterpillars and butterflies, we can also think about Easter. First, a caterpillar spins a chrysalis or cocoon. After a while a butterfly hatches and comes out. This reminds us that Jesus was in the tomb. After three days, He came out of the tomb alive.

Use the small grid as a guide to help you make a butterfly. Some of the squares have been divided in half with a diagonal black line. Count across and down the grid to find the same square on your grid. Draw a black line on your grid to match each one, then follow the code to color each square.

	1	2	3	4	5	6	7	8
A	B/Y	Y/ B	B	B	B	B	B/ Y	Y/ B
B	Y	Y	Y/ B	B/ P	P /B	B/ Y	Y	Y
C	Y	Y	Y	Y/ P	P /Y	Y	Y	Y
D	B/ Y	Y	Y	Y/ P	P /Y	Y	Y	Y/ B
E	B/ Y	Y	Y	P	P	Y	Y	Y/ B
F	Y	Y	Y	P	P	Y	Y	Y
G	B/ Y	Y	Y/ B	B/ P	P /B	B/ Y	Y	Y/ B

Y=Yellow   B=Blue   P=Purple

He lives, He lives, who once was dead.

	1	2	3	4	5	6	7	8
A								
B								
C								
D								
E								
F								
G								

How would you have felt if you had been there too?

Early at the Tomb

On the first Easter morning, three women came to the tomb. They were bringing spices to get the body of Jesus ready to be buried. They knew that the stone in front of the tomb was very heavy. They wondered who would move the stone so they could go inside the tomb.

What a surprise they had! When they arrived, they discovered the stone had already been rolled away. An angel was inside. Follow the color code to find the angel in the tomb.

= YELLOW + GRAY △ GREEN • WHITE □ BROWN

He Is Risen

Fear and Joy

When the women saw the angel, they were surprised and frightened. "Don't be afraid," the angel told them. "You are looking for Jesus, but He is not here."

Fill in the blanks to discover the rest of the angel's message. Find the words on the petals of the flower that match each number. Write the words that match the numbers in each blank.

Have no fear.
Your Savior is
near.

"___ ___   ___ ___ ___   ___ ___ ___   ___ ___ ___ ___.
  1   2   3   4

___ ___   ___ ___ ___   ___ ___ ___ ___." Matthew 28:6a
  5   6   7

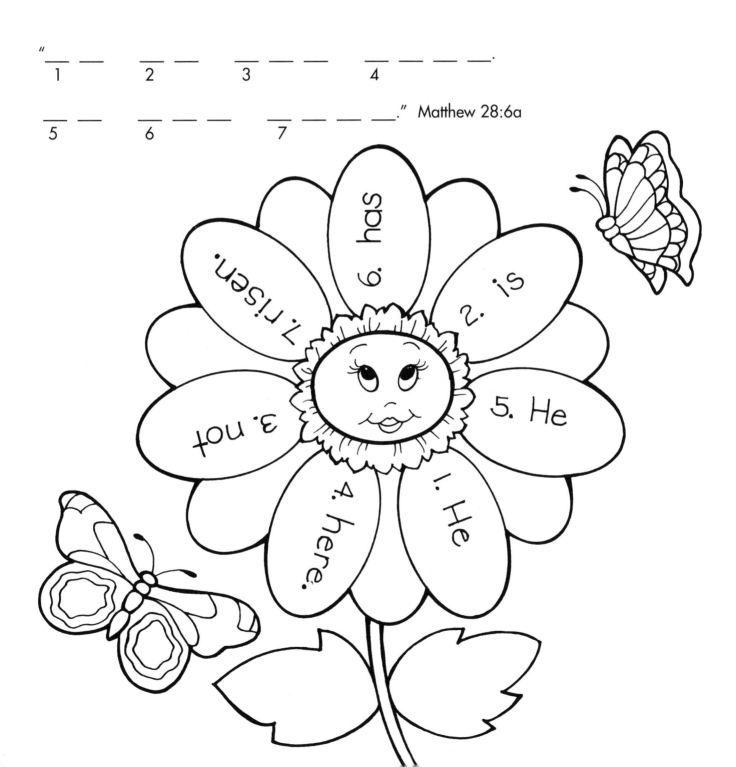

Write the angel's words.

Have No Fear

The angel told the women, "Do not be afraid, for I know that you are looking for Jesus, who was crucified. He is not here; He has risen, just as He said. Come and see the place where He lay" (Matthew 28:5–6).

Follow the code to uncover some of the angel's words. Look at each picture, and write the first letter of its name on the blank above. When you are finished, write the angel's words into the speech balloon.

Write the first letter of each picture.

(Pictures, in order: hat, egg, hat, apple, star, rose, igloo, star, egg, nose.

Go and Tell

The women were so excited to hear that Jesus was alive. The angel told them to go and tell the good news to the disciples. Follow the maze to help the women find the disciples. What do you think they told them? What would you have told the disciples about Jesus?

Who can you tell about Jesus?

START

END

Make your own Easter story book.

Make and Tell

The women told their friends about Jesus. Now you can make a book to help you tell the wonderful story of Easter to one of your friends.

Have an adult make a photocopy of this page. Color the pictures and cut the book out along the solid black lines. Fold the book along the horizontal dotted line, and then fold it along the vertical dotted line. Give your book to a friend.

More to do: Write and draw your own pictures on a piece of paper and make it into an Easter book.

The First Easter

Jesus rose from the dead. My Savior lives!

Jesus died on the cross to forgive our sins.

Jesus was buried. Three days later ...

Share the News

The women told the disciples what they had seen and heard. What can you tell someone else about Jesus? Who needs to hear the Good News?

Use the lines on the Easter butterfly to write a letter to someone. Share what the resurrection of Jesus means to you.

Use this butterfly to write an Easter letter.

What did Jesus do for you?

An Empty Tomb

Two disciples of Jesus, Peter and John, ran to the tomb. Peter went into the tomb and saw the pieces of cloth that had been around Jesus. John came in after him and saw that the tomb was empty. The Bible tells us that John believed. (See John 20:8.)

Follow the code to find out what we can believe about Jesus.

A	D	E	F	G	H	I	H	M	N	O	R	S	T	Y
15	14	13	12	11	10	9	8	7	6	5	4	3	2	1

__ __ __ __ __   __ __ __ __ __   __ __ __ __ __
5 6 2 8 13   2 10 9 4 14   14 15 1 10 13

__ __ __ __ __   __ __ __ __ __   __ __ __ __   __ __ __
15 4 5 3 13   15 11 15 9 6   12 4 5 7   2 10 13

__ __ __ __ .
14 13 15 14

Mary Sees an Angel

Mary Magdalene came to the tomb. As she looked inside, she saw two angels in white. What do you think the angels looked like? Draw two angels inside the tomb. Color the rest of the picture and add some Easter flowers.

How do you think Mary felt?

Jesus Speaks to Mary

When Mary was at the tomb, she started to cry. She knew Jesus was gone and she did not understand why. "Why are you crying?" the angels asked. Mary answered, "Because they have taken away my Lord, and I do not know where they have put Him."

Someone came and stood behind Mary. Who do you think it was? Follow the dots to find out.

Jesus is with you today.

Mary Recognizes the Lord

Mary thought Jesus was a man who worked in the garden. She asked if he had taken Jesus away. The man behind her said, "Mary." Mary turned around and said, "Master." The man behind her was Jesus, and now she knew He was alive.

Make a stand-up picture to remind you that Jesus is alive for you too. Have an adult make a photocopy of this page. Color the picture and cut it out. Fold along the dotted lines. Glue the two sides together at the tab. Stand the picture up in a special place.

Make your own stand-up picture.

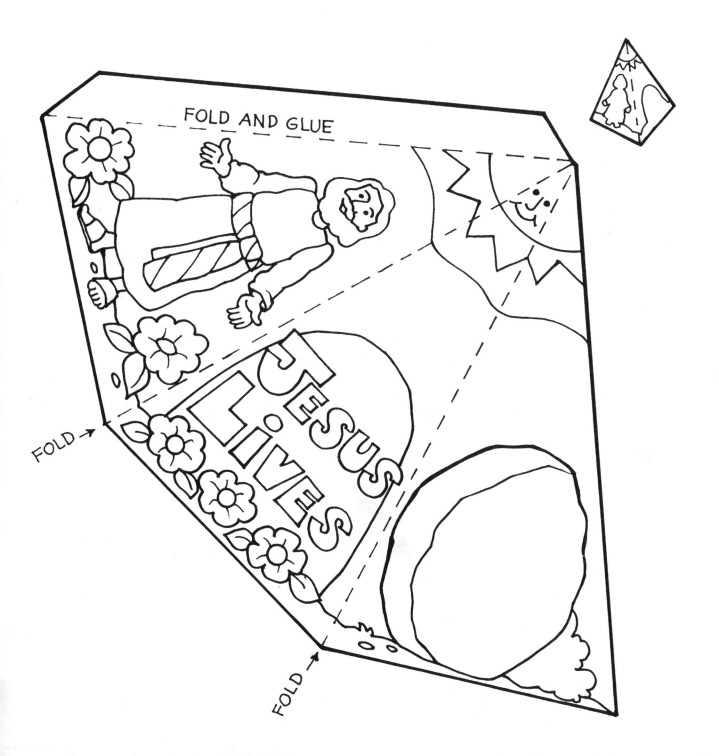

FOLD AND GLUE

FOLD →

JESUS LIVES

← FOLD

Design your own Easter necklace.

The Other Women See Jesus

Jesus met the other women on their way to see the disciples. Jesus said, "Don't be afraid. Go, tell My brothers that they should go into Galilee. They will see Me there." The women were happy and went with joy to tell the disciples their news.

Make an Easter necklace to use in sharing the story of Jesus' love. Make a photocopy of this page. Color the eggs and the butterfly. Cut them out and punch a hole in each one. String a piece of yarn through each hole to make a necklace. String pieces of pasta or round cereal between the eggs and the butterfly to complete your necklace.

He Lives

or

He Lives

On the Way to Emmaus

That night two disciples were walking to the little town of Emmaus. They talked as they walked. As they were talking, a stranger came and began to walk with them. Follow the maze to help the men walk to Emmaus.

Jesus walks with you today.

START

EMMAUS

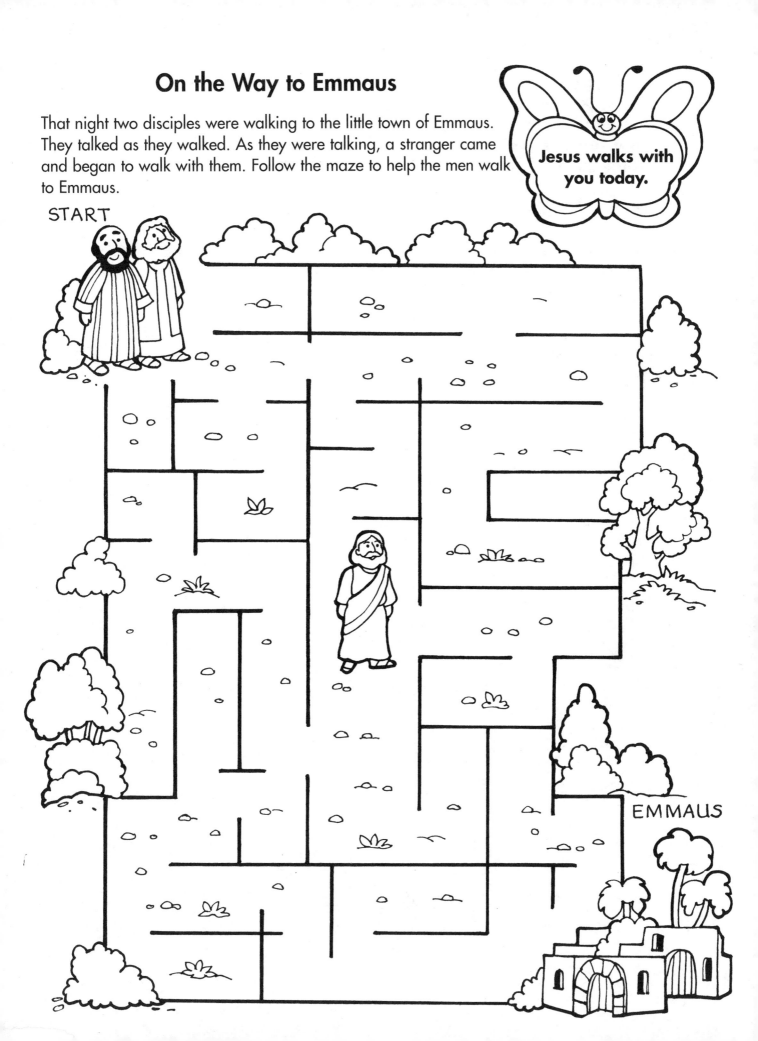

Draw a picture of your favorite Bible story.

Why Jesus Came

The stranger walked with the two men. He asked them why they were sad. The men told the stranger all about their friend Jesus who had died on the cross. The stranger told the two men what God's Word said about the Savior who would have to die and rise again.

The story of Jesus' saving love is in the Bible for all of us to read and hear. Finish the dot-to-dot to draw the Bible. Connect the smaller black dots to trace over the Bible verse. Memorize the Bible verse and say it often. Tell it to a friend.

He died for all

2 Corinthians 5:14

Stay With Us

When the two men arrived at Emmaus, they invited the stranger to stay and eat with them. During the meal, the stranger blessed the bread. The men suddenly knew that the stranger was Jesus. Jesus disappeared, and the men hurried back to Jerusalem.

Copy the picture from the small grid onto the big grid. Color the picture.

More to do: Make a photocopy of the picture, cut it out, and glue it onto a piece of construction paper. Punch holes around the sides and lace the picture. Hang it on your wall.

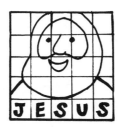

In Him is gladness!

Easter Joy

After Jesus had left them the men remembered how their hearts were filled with joy as He talked with them. Our hearts can be filled with joy because Jesus died and rose for us.

Follow the code to color this Easter message. After coloring the red and yellow spaces, use other bright colors to finish the picture. What happy thoughts about Jesus fill your heart with joy?

X = Red   ● = Yellow

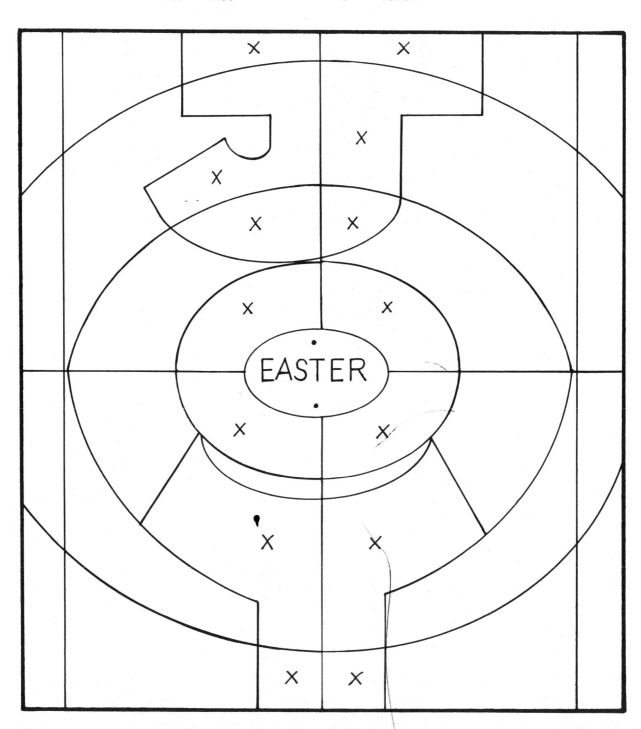

The Lord is With You

The disciples could see Jesus and know that He was alive and that He was with them. Even though you cannot see Him, you can know that Jesus is always with you.

Make a doorknob hanger to remind you that Jesus is with you day and night. Have an adult make a photocopy of this page. Color the door hanger and cut it out. Be sure to cut on all the lines, even around the circle. Hang it on the doorknob of your bedroom door.

At home, away, Jesus is always with you.

CUT

CUT OUT

I am with you always.

You need not fear if Jesus is near.

The Lord Lives

Jesus came to see the disciples where they were hiding. When they saw Him, they were afraid He was a ghost. Jesus showed them His hands and feet, and He even ate some fish to show them He was not a ghost.

Do you know what Jesus said to His disciples? Use a dark color to fill in all the spaces marked with a dot. Write the word you find in the space provided. Use bright colors to fill in the other spaces too.

" __ __ __ __ __ be with you,"

Jesus told His friends.

Thomas Believes

Thomas was not with the other disciples when Jesus came to see them. He did not believe Jesus was alive. One week later, Jesus came back to see the disciples. This time Thomas was with them.

Follow the code to find out what Thomas said to Jesus and what Jesus said to Thomas.

We believe even though we do not see Jesus.

B D E I L G N O R S V

My _ _ _ _
and my _ _ _ .

Blessed are those who have not _ _ _ _ and yet have _ _ _ _ _ _ _ _ .

Jesus can do anything.

At the Sea

After Easter, the friends of Jesus went out in a boat to fish. They tried and tried, but they could not catch any fish. Jesus stood by the shore, but His friends did not know it was Him. He told them, "Throw your net on the other side of the boat." The men did this, and they caught so many fish that their nets started to break.

Draw lots of fish in the net. Use colors or markers to add sunshine and some clouds to the sky. Draw a campfire on the shore next to Jesus where they can cook the fish and enjoy breakfast together.

Jesus Forgives

After they caught the fish, Peter jumped into the water and hurried to Jesus. They cooked the fish, and Jesus ate breakfast with His friends. While they were eating, Jesus assured Peter that He forgave him for saying that he did not know Jesus. Jesus forgives us, too, when we do things we should not do.

Follow the maze to help Peter get from the boat to Jesus.

Jesus forgives you too.

JESUS   ← END   START   PETER

Praise the Lord.

Alleluia

On Easter morning we sing songs of praise to Jesus, our risen Savior. We use the word "Alleluia" to show our joy. Sing the words from this song using the melody for "Twinkle, Twinkle Little Star."

**"Alleluia!" let us sing
Unto Christ, our risen King.
Every girl and every boy,
Praise the Lord with songs of joy.
"Alleluia!" let us sing
Unto Christ, our risen King.**

Choose a melody and write your own song using a favorite melody. Sing it with your family.

Easter Word Search

Find and circle each word in the Word Box. Be sure to look up and down, back and forth until you find each one. Cross out each word as you find it. What part of the Easter story do you remember when you see each word? How many other Easter words can you think of? Can you make your own word search?

May the joy of Easter be with you always.

Word Box

Angel	Arisen	Disciples	Grave	Jesus
John	Mary	Peter	Soldiers	Stone	Women

S E L P I C S I D

O J E S U S P T Q

L X G R A V E H N

D Y N H O J T O E

I M A R Y X E M M

E Z N E S I R A O

R N Y E N O T S W

S A M O H T P W V

Make an Easter egg tree.

An Egg Tree

For a long time eggs have been used at Easter to help people remember the resurrection of Jesus. Use bright colors to decorate the eggs on this Easter egg tree. Think about how happy you are that Jesus is alive.

More to do: Make a photocopy of this page. Color the eggs and cut them out. Punch a hole at the top of each egg. Tie yarn through the holes and hang the eggs on a tree branch that has been set into a jar filled with rocks. Enjoy your colorful Easter egg tree.

A Special Easter Basket

Share your Easter joy with others. Make a special Easter basket to help you remember what Jesus did for you on the first Easter. Give your basket to someone who needs to feel the joy of Easter.

Make a photocopy of this page. Use bright colors to show how happy you feel that Jesus died and rose again for you. Add flowers and other decorations. Cut it out on the solid lines and fold it on the dotted lines. Glue the cross on the back of the basket. Add Easter grass and candy. You can even add some Bible verses to the basket.

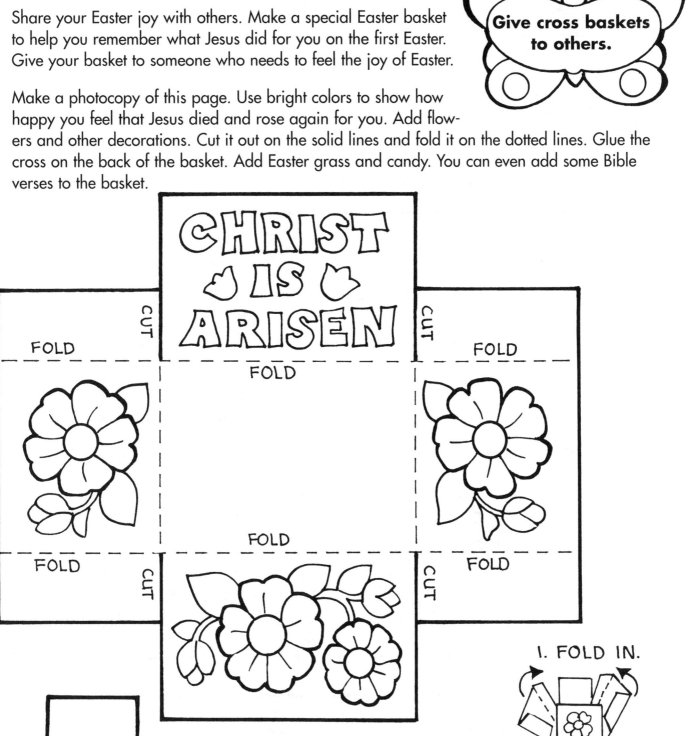

Give cross baskets to others.

CHRIST IS ARISEN

CUT
FOLD
CUT
FOLD

FOLD

FOLD

FOLD

FOLD
FOLD
CUT

GLUE TAB

1. FOLD IN.

2. GLUE DOWN TABS.

3. GLUE ON CROSS.

CHRIST IS ARISEN

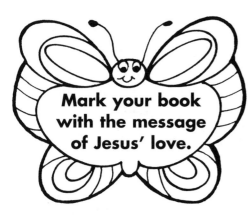

Search the Scriptures

In the Bible we learn many things about the saving love of Jesus. Make these Easter bookmarks. Use one for yourself and share the others with someone else.

Make a photocopy of this page. Color the bookmarks and cut them out.

More to do: Glue the bookmarks on pieces of colorful construction paper, poster board, or ribbon. Cover them with clear plastic adhesive so they will not tear.

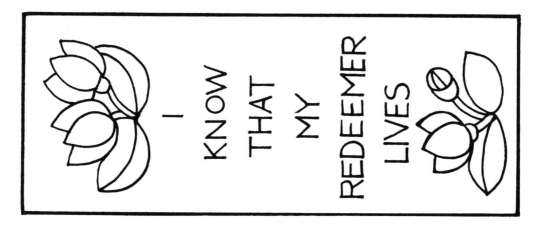

An Easter Greeting

Sometimes Christians use the words of the angel in the tomb to greet one another. Read the words upside down and backwards. Write them in the spaces below. Use these words to say hello to your family and friends at Easter.

He is risen for you!

HE IS RISEN.

HE IS RISEN INDEED.

___ ___ _ ___ ___ ___ ___ ___ ___.

___ ___ _ ___ ___ ___ ___ ___ ___ ___ ___ ___ ___.

A Butterfly Easter Bonnet

Share and wear your Easter joy.

All believers will have new life in heaven because Jesus died and rose again. Sometimes Christians wear new clothes at Easter to celebrate the new life they have in Jesus. Sometimes they even wear a special Easter bonnet.

Make this Alleluia Easter bonnet to celebrate the resurrection of Jesus. Have an adult photocopy this page. Color the letters and decorate the butterfly. Punch holes in each side. Tie a piece of elastic cord or yarn through each hole. Tie the strings behind your head. Or, glue the butterfly bonnet to a strip of paper cut to fit your head.

Celebrate Easter! Celebrate Jesus!

ALLE LUIA